Ezekiel J. Donnell

Slavery and Protection

Ezekiel J. Donnell

Slavery and Protection

ISBN/EAN: 9783744737210

Printed in Europe, USA, Canada, Australia, Japan

Cover: Foto ©ninafisch / pixelio.de

More available books at **www.hansebooks.com**

SLAVERY AND "PROTECTION";

An Historical Review and Appeal to the Workshop and the Farm.

BY

E. J. DONNELL.

NEW YORK:
E. J. DONNELL, 2 & 4 STONE STREET.
1882.

SLAVERY AND "PROTECTION":

An Historical Review and Appeal to the Workshop and the Farm.

BY

E. J. DONNELL.

New York:
E. J. DONNELL, 2 & 4 STONE STREET.
1882.

Digitized by the Internet Archive
in 2011 with funding from
The Institute of Museum and Library Services through an Indiana State Library LSTA Grant

http://www.archive.org/details/slaveryprotectiodonn

PREFACE.

BEING requested by the New York Free Trade Club to read to them this essay, I wrote the following, which served to introduce it, and will also answer for a preface:

"I was induced to write the short essay I am about to read to you by a desire to gather up some neglected threads in the tariff question which seem to have escaped from the observation of others.

"During forty years I have been a careful observer of all social and political movements and tendencies everywhere, but especially in this country. I have always aimed at getting beneath the surface of events, and if possible to see and understand the play of those subtle, but all-powerful forces, which govern all phenomena, yet escape general observation.

"As a philosophical and psychological study the history of the United States is unique. The history of the world is full of examples of nations and peoples who have toiled for centuries, groping in darkness and slavery, to find their way at last into some degree of light and liberty.

"The United States, on the other hand, started as a nation, with the very loftiest ideals of liberty and justice embodied in its official documents and fundamental law. Yet from the very birth of the Nation it has been forced to contend with all the old forms of selfishness, which in all ages have corrupted peoples, and sapped the foundations of government.

"Generally the ideal standard of right has been held aloft somewhere in the field of battle; but there have been times when it required true insight and profound faith to believe it was not fated to go down forever. In nothing have the people and the government wandered further from the original ideal than in taxation. In the 'protective' system all the principles of liberty and equality have been trampled under foot as contemptuously as could have been the case in any nation that had never seen the light!

"The reflections and emotions excited by these facts are partially expressed in the essay I am about to read.

"The present commanding position of the physical sciences has, in my opinion, injuriously affected the spirit and methods of political economists. As I regard it, economical science is pre-eminently ethical, and inseparable from a true science of mind. This view has, in part, guided my treatment of the subject.

"The way in which the working people of this, so-called, enlightened country have been hoodwinked and shorn like lambs by ignorant and selfish protectionists has pained and excited my mind for years. It seemed to me at times impossible to remain silent. At last I resolved to give expression to my feelings in some form, even if it must be in defiance of all the conventional rules of composition."

I.
NATURAL AND HISTORICAL CONNECTION OF SLAVERY AND "PROTECTION."

In the history of Europe and America since the accession of Charles V. to the throne of Spain in 1517 few facts are so conspicuous, and at the same time so little noticed by historians, as the connection between modern, that is, African slavery, and the modern system of protective legislation in trade and navigation. Both these systems originated in the demoniac brain of Charles. In 1519 he was elected Emperor of Germany, in 1522 he issued to a Flemish merchant the first government license to import Africans as slaves into the Spanish-American colonies. The trade was rapidly organized, as well as legalized, on a large scale.

The protective system he adopted was based upon what is now known as the balance of trade. It was known at one time in Europe as Colbertism, then as the mercantile system. Its policy was to discourage imports; to sell as much as possible to foreigners, and to buy as little as possible from them. By this policy Charles supposed that Spain, owning, as she did, the rich American mines, could monopolize the precious metals.

The philosophy of this dual policy of slavery and

"protection," if correctly formulated, would be about as follows: If one people can relieve themselves from the necessity of labor by enslaving another people, the benefit accruing to the one will be equal to the injury inflicted on the other!

If you are trading freely with a neighboring people, both parties fairly dividing the profits, then by destroying half this trade you will be able to monopolize all the profit for yourselves! The moral of this is (I beg you will mark it well), IGNORANCE AND SELFISHNESS ARE TWIN BROTHERS.

Let us take a short glance at the condition in which Charles found Europe, and the condition in which he left it.

In the eleventh century we have the first faint indications of intellectual awakening in the European mind. Then, as always, it was manifested in industrial activity. In the twelfth century this became quite marked everywhere, from Italy to the Baltic.

Unfortunately for the commercial cities of northern Italy they were rivals and nearly always at war with each other. Still their industrial and commercial success was immense. It penetrated everywhere, from England to India.

The Free Cities of the North were in some respects more fortunate than their Southern sisters. They were in the midst of a semi-barbarous people. Union among themselves was a necessity; hence the Hanseatic League, which was organized in the last years of the twelfth or first years of the thirteenth century. It soon numbered about eighty cities besides confederates. In this great confederation were centred all the forces that were destined to redeem Europe from barbarism. From it, as from the heart, civilization flowed out into all the veins and arteries of commerce. Out of this friendly contact arose commerce of ideas, which is the essence of all commerce.

In two hundred and fifty years the mission of the Hanseatic League was accomplished. Piracy on land and sea was extirpated; institutions of learning were established everywhere; law was substituted for force —slavery was dying out. The conquests of commerce over barbarism and over ignorance went hand in hand. Commercial enterprise was the offspring of intellectual enterprise. The art of printing was discovered—the mariner's compass was invented. The human mind revelled in its victories when it conquered the earth by its geographical, and the heavens by its astronomical discoveries.

It is the opinion of the best historical writers on political economy, that the whole tendency of Europe at the time of the discovery of America in 1492 was toward commercial freedom. Spain began to get her American possessions into working order when Charles came upon the field, like a demon of discord.

To the extremest ignorance of the sixth century he added the positive intellectual force of the sixteenth.

He was a native of Flanders. From the first he exploited the jealousy felt by the Northern commercial cities toward the Italian. He extinguished the liberties of the Italian cities in blood, and strangled their trade with the hangman's rope of "protection." It required three hundred years for them to recover sufficient vitality to pulsate visibly.

The study of economy as a science, beyond some Italian works on finance, had not begun; consequently the system of Charles was not met by other nations in the spirit of economical science, but in the spirit of retaliation and war. The whole of Europe engaged in the slave-trade, and in the policy of injuring each other's commerce as much as possible. Europe and America were a pandemonium. No human being can form any adequate idea of the horrors of the slave-trade. The native tribes of Africa were everywhere at war to obtain captives to sell to the slave-traders for rum. It is certain that many were killed for every one that was captured. The cruel mortality of the " middle passage " whitened a lane across the basin of the Atlantic with human bones. When the remnant arrived in the colonies they were guarded by bloodhounds, and governed by the lash and by torture.

During nearly three hundred years after the accession of Charles an average of one year in four was spent by the colonial powers of Europe in prosecuting wars wholly commercial in their origin, and one year more in wars partially or indirectly so. Their whole policy may be summed up in one sentence, in the language of Blanqui, the historian of Political Economy: "They used the colonists to rob the natives, and tariffs to rob the colonists." The effect of this policy on Spain, the chief criminal, is a not unfair gauge of its general influence. In fifty years after Charles' accession the vitality of Spain was wasting away, her industry was ruined.

Seville, which in 1519 counted 16,000 silk workshops employing 130,000 workmen, had only 405 manufactories.

Segovia, in which formerly 25,000 pieces were annually produced, made in 1579 only 400 pieces.

In fifty years more Spain had sunk into the depths of poverty and degradation. From the highest grandeur of empire to the lowest condition of imbecility inside of a single century! Nothing like it is recorded in history.

Many historians are pleased to ascribe all this to the religious frenzy that possessed the Spanish people for some centuries. I have no wish to underestimate the influence of such aberrations; but I have no hesitation in asserting that with intelligent liberty in industry such insane intolerance could not have coexisted. Friendly intercourse through free trade is death to intolerance. The direct contact with cause and effect has a sure healing influence on all such dementia, whether political or religious.

In the eighteenth century the situation became intolerable. The condition of the masses was such that it is doubtful if there was any alternative between revolution and such depopulation as took place in the middle ages. Before these conditions ripened into the French Revolution, the colonial system, which was closely connected with them in its genesis and development, came to an end by the revolt of the British colonies, now the United States.

Literature had ceased to devote itself exclusively to theology, and had plunged into philosophical speculations and political discussions with a boldness and self-assertion never before known.

It is sufficient for my present purpose to state that all the essential principles of the ripest political philosophy of the eighteenth century were embodied in our Declaration of Independence.

After independence was achieved and the Representatives of the people met in convention to form a constitutional union, these twin relics of barbarism, slavery and "protection," appeared in their halls and distracted their councils—alternately begging and threatening, as they continued to do afterward; one of them for three quarters of a century, and the other up to the present time.

There was a rich "placer" in the new nation. Three millions of brave, intelligent people, masters of their own destiny, with a whole continent behind them teeming with wealth, and waiting for the husbandman and the miner. People willing to earn an honest living by honest work were grateful to the Almighty Giver of all good for this splendid heritage, and felt that all they wanted from government was protection from violence. The majority of the people at that time had a wholesome dread of too much government.

There was another element in the population with different views entirely. They had no desire to work; they greatly preferred living by their wits.

These fertile lands, and rich mines, and strong workmen could stand a good deal of bleeding and pillage without so much as knowing how it was done; and after all be better off than any other laborers in the world!

You see Nature always creates a portion of the human family to work for the whole, and another portion for ornament perhaps.

With these views slavery and "protection" entered the constitutional convention, covered all over with crime and dripping with blood!

In the face of the then recent Declaration of Independence, with its organ-notes of freedom still rolling through the nations, concealments were necessary, and they were resorted to without scruple!

Slavery said: "We have no expectation of lasting long. Treat us with gentleness and forbearance; give us what we want for the present, and we will surely disappear in time, without giving the slightest trouble to anybody."

"Protection" said: "We only want a start. We cannot compete with the organization and capital of England, who, being defeated in war, will try to crush our rising industry! Many manufactures are already in a healthy condition, but we want some guarantee of government aid to make sure that our arch-enemy across the water does not waylay and destroy us."

Slavery and *"Protection"* were always true patriots? Their voices always rose above all others when the country was in danger from English intrigues! On the one hand the word was given, "British abolitionism;" it was echoed on the other by "British free trade!" You perceive these two patriots had equal *respect for the intelligence of their countrymen!* They had good reason, as you will see.

They put in their claims simultaneously. From complaisance they suddenly resorted to threats. The South declared that it would not join the Union if the importation of slaves from Africa was prohibited. New England scouted the idea that she had any use for the Union at all, unless her shipping was protected by a navigation act. She needed no Union to protect her from war; she was able to protect herself!

These two great interests must be conciliated somehow, or all hope for union was at an end! How was it to be done?

The men who signed the Declaration of Independence could not consent to put slavery in the Constitution; yet something must be done somehow. Mark the result. The Constitution was so worded that, some centuries hence, when posterity reads the document, it will be impossible for it to discover from the contents that slavery existed under it. Yet it was agreed that slavery should be protected by it *through interpretation*. That was, at least, the tacit understanding.

The same course, precisely, was pursued toward the

other claimant. Neither slavery nor "protection" could get what it demanded without violating the principles of justice and liberty. This they would not consent to do in the letter of the Constitution; but they did consent that it should be done by interpretation until the progress of liberty should grow up to the letter of the Constitution, and thus furnish the correct interpretation. Let us now see what was the phraseology in the constitutional provision under which Congress assumed the power of discriminating taxation.

Article I. Section 8: "The Congress shall have power TO LAY AND COLLECT TAXES, duties, imposts, and excises, to pay the debts and provide for the common defence and general welfare of the United States. But all duties, imposts, and excises shall be uniform throughout the United States.

"To regulate Commerce with Foreign Nations and among the several States and with the Indian tribes."

Now look for a moment what Congress has been doing under the powers granted to it by this section of the Constitution.

It began by levying import duties averaging 8½ per cent, discriminating in favor of a few pet industries at the expense of all the others! This was only the thin edge of the wedge. It was sufficient to admit any practicable extreme.

At one time during the past twenty years import duties averaged 50 per cent on the total imports. Now, this tax is so levied that the government collects two hundred millions, and a thousand millions are not collected by the government at all, but go into the hands of manufacturing monopolists, who are protected from foreign competition by the government. For instance:

Eleven rich corporations make one million tons of steel rails on which the import duty would be twenty-eight millions. The cost of importation, including freight, would doubtless be seven millions more, making in all thirty-five millions. Less than one sixth of this amount is paid by these corporations for labor, at rates of wages not much more than half what less skilful labor could earn on Western lands!

Another instance:

A bounty of five and one half millions, in the form of a tariff, is given to a few Louisiana planters for turning the finest cotton lands on the globe into third-rate sugar plantations. In order to arrive at this *splendid economical result*, and, if possible, TO DIVIDE THE SOUTH ON THE TARIFF QUESTION, fifty millions per annum in duties are paid on imported sugar.

This growth of the protective fallacy had an almost exact parallel in the progress of slavery up to 1860. From a not unreasonable demand for protection to vested interests it grew up to a demand, practically, for dictatorial powers in the whole policy and management of the government! Nor was this enough; it assumed to dictate to universal suffrage!

Slavery, no longer content with toleration, asserted its right to be treated as a part of the Divine order! Having no recognition in the written Constitution, it obtained through interpretation by the Supreme Court a full recognition of its most extreme demands!

IN THE SAME LINE, "PROTECTION," WITHOUT AUTHORITY IN THE CONSTITUTION TO LEVY ANY TAX THAT THE GOVERNMENT DOES NOT COLLECT, AND THAT IS NOT NECESSARY TO PAY ITS DEBT AND EXPENSES, ACTUALLY, AND WITHOUT DISGUISE, USES ITS UTMOST INGENUITY TO SO LEVY TAXES, IN A WAY THAT WILL BRING TO THE GOVERNMENT THE SMALLEST POSSIBLE REVENUE, AND TO FAVORED INDUSTRIES THE LARGEST. NOR IS THIS ENOUGH; IMPORTS CANNOT BE KEPT DOWN PERMANENTLY BY ANY TARIFF, UNLESS EXPORTS ARE KEPT DOWN TO THE SAME LEVEL; HENCE THE PRESENT INCREASE OF REVENUE PRODUCING A LARGE SURPLUS NOTWITHSTANDING THE INFERNAL DEVICES OF CONGRESS AND THE LOBBIES. CONGRESS, DRIVEN TO ITS LAST RESOURCES, ADOPTS THE DESPERATE EXPEDIENT OF ATTEMPTING TO BRIBE THE PEOPLE WITH THEIR OWN MONEY, IN APPROPRIATIONS. IN THE MEAN TIME THEY APPOINT A TARIFF COMMISSION TO GAIN DELAY, AND TO MAKE A REPORT TO CONGRESS ADVISING ANOTHER "KANSAS NEBRASKA BILL WITH A STUMP SPEECH IN ITS BELLY;"—I quote from Benton.

The parallel does not stop here. As in 1856, when both the great political parties were almost equally frightened at the idea of opposing slavery, so now, even the once great party, whose greatness was built upon its supposed love of liberty, in trade and everything else, is painfully astraddle of the fence, balancing itself on a very rough and uncomfortable rail! Thrown into a *negative condition of mind* by the failure of its pro-slavery philosophy, it has never, so far, recovered the entire use of its faculties. Its supreme desire seems to have been to get into office; and in its *demented condition* it supposed the Republican party owed its success to its vices!—to its violations of liberty and justice, instead of its advocacy of them, as it did in fact. One step further, and you will see the parallel is complete.

No Dred Scott decision can be procured from the Supreme Court, but the president of the tariff commission announces that the principle of "protection" is no longer in question! HENCEFORWARD "PROTECTION" IS NO LONGER A DOCTRINE; IT IS A DOGMA.

All great controversies proceed thus. From false premises falsehood advances step by step to logical and generally to dogmatic conclusions. At this point the revolt begins: at first as silent but as powerful as gravitation; in the end as terrible as an earthquake.

The master-passion of that Divine emanation which we call soul is love of truth; when by relentless logic this is attacked in its citadel, the Almighty himself defends!

THIS VILE CREATURE, "PROTECTION," IS CHAINED TO THE DEAD BODY OF SLAVERY, AND IT WILL BE BURIED IN THE SAME GRAVE. AS IT NEVER HAS HAD A SOUL THERE IS NO DANGER OF ANY RESURRECTION.

II.

"PROTECTION" THE SOURCE OF CORRUPTION IN POLITICS AND IMBECILITY IN INDUSTRY.

HONEST Horace Greeley was of the opinion that "protection" to American industry achieved a great victory in the overthrow of slavery, and contributed not a little to that end.

I have no disposition to dispute the accuracy of his opinion. I am inclined to think it has some foundation in truth; but if so, I fear the people only changed masters.

So far as slavery and "protection" were concerned, it was a contest for power.

The blacks have been freed in one form, but both whites and blacks have been enslaved in another.

In every contest for power during some centuries past one or the other party has used and abused the sacred name of Liberty; and when Liberty has accepted the alliance of either, she has always been betrayed.

The lesson of history, emphasized again and again, is that Liberty needs to beware of her allies. When victory inclines to her side knaves flock to her standard from all quarters.

It is certain that when slavery retired from the halls of Congress, and sent its armies into the field, the "protectionists" did not limit their *patriotic* efforts to volunteering for enlistment in the army. They attacked the tariff with much more promptness and persistence than they did the enemy's battalions.

For nearly ten years after the Morrill tariff passed Congress in 1861, one amendment followed another, all increasing duties on imports and with the evident purpose of so complicating the whole process of getting merchandise through the Custom-house as to discourage imports by self-respecting merchants. In many cases the smuggler ran less risk than the regular merchant, so adroitly was the law framed to catch the unwary.

Of course it was prohibition the "protectionists" meant, but they dared not say so.

They framed the law as they framed the Constitution, with an after-thought—with a purpose that they dared not avow.

This policy has now lasted about twenty-one years.

During fourteen years previous to 1861 we had what is called a revenue tariff. This places the two systems on exhibition for purposes of comparison.

The duties under Robert J. Walker's tariff of 1846 averaged twenty per cent. The rapid expansion of trade and consequent increase of revenue enabled Congress to reduce the rate to about fourteen per cent in 1856. This was the lowest tariff since that of Alexander Hamilton.

It should be remembered that discriminating taxation is only one of the forms of the protective system. The other forms consist mainly in discriminating appropriations of the common wealth.

It is impossible permanently to separate them. The one suggests, if it does not necessitate the other.

If the order of natural law in the production and distribution of wealth can be improved by legislation, it is the obvious duty of government to pursue the system to its logical results.

Of course the government owns nothing. It has nothing to give the people but what it takes from them. What it gives to one part of the people, it must take from another part.

The whole experiment has been tried, almost without check, certainly without effective opposition, for twenty years.

Rarely in the history of the world has any experiment in legislation had such a favorable field to work in.

No possible amount of bad legislation could entirely neutralize the wealth-producing power of this country.

Hitherto the party in power has always been more or less successful in claiming credit for the rapid progress of the country in wealth and population. Hence it is that the absorbing purpose of all parties is, by any means or all means, to obtain power.

SOUND, SCIENTIFIC LEGISLATION HAS ALWAYS BEEN THE OFFSPRING OF POVERTY; BAD LEGISLATION, OF SUPERABUNDANT WEALTH.

Great changes have taken place in the last twenty years, almost unobserved by the multitude. The generation to which the practical working of an opposite policy was known by personal observation, is rapidly passing away. As one of them I will venture to record a few of the facts, with the impressions they have produced on my mind.

It is evident that a great change has taken place in the distribution of wealth. I suppose there are a hundred, perhaps hundreds of persons in this country to-day worth a million and over, where there was one in 1860. Thoughtless people think this a sign of prosperity; yet all history teaches us that it is a sure indication of rottenness somewhere, especially when accompanied by other facts which I will point out hereafter.

Previous to 1860 street-begging was almost entirely unknown among us. This was a just cause of pride to Americans, and of admiring surprise on the part of foreigners. Every thoughtful European who travelled in this country, no matter how unfriendly, from Marryat to Dickens, made this acknowledgment ungrudgingly.

The word *tramp*, in the sense in which it is now used almost exclusively in the United States, is not yet fifteen years old. The latest edition of Webster does not give the new definition.

It may be remembered that when the panic took place in 1873 nearly all the protected industries collapsed like a house of cards. The operatives were driven into the streets and highways to beg or steal for a living. If their employers had accumulated wealth, as many of them had, they did not feel bound by any *conventional law of morals*, or any known principle of economics, to share it with their employés. The government had built the house of cards at the public expense. Their intentions were good, no doubt. They might use the common wealth in indirect appropriations to special industries, as *experiments in political economy*, but to rescue the innocent victims of their mistake by any appropriations of money from the public treasury did not seem to them to be *good politics;* and, if they in fact weighed the question at all, such a conclusion would be generally admitted to be perfectly sound. It is not improbable that, in point of fact, they were like children playing with a steam-engine in a factory, accidentally setting a houseful of machinery in motion, without being able to comprehend either the cause or the consequences.

However this may have been, our country has been furnished with just cause for shame and patriotic humiliation.

Previous to 1860 we had experienced several severe revulsions in trade. That of 1837 was accompanied by an almost universal collapse of the currency, so that the very machinery by means of which modern commerce can alone be conducted was smashed to pieces. There was much poverty consequent, but no want, and no degrading beggary and vagabondism. How is it now?

I wish to be moderate; yet it is difficult to suppress indignation on such a subject. I verily believe that this country has, in the last twenty years, made more millionaires and paupers than any country in history. There is, perhaps, one parallel; Rome in the last years of the Republic, when the Roman oligarchy " pumped the shores of the Mediterranean dry," and thus prepared the people for the usurpation of the Cæsars.

Street-begging has not yet ripened into a trade, such as it is in Southern Europe. We have no class corresponding to the "jolly beggars" of Naples. Most of those we meet in our streets have an expression of sadness and shrinking shame terribly painful to look at. I feel very sure that if the American people would only pause long enough in their headlong rush of business to think of this subject, some adequate remedy would soon be applied. The cause at least would be removed; and the true cause is not difficult to discover, if people would only shut their ears for a while, and open their eyes. I have boundless confidence in the good sense and sound conscience of the American people when their attention is fairly directed to questions appealing to these qualities. They may be deceived by selfish people for a time, but not always.

Students of what has been called political economy have always insisted that protective legislation in any form reduces the aggregate wealth-producing power of the nation.

The free-trade arguments on this point have never been answered directly; but abstract reasoning has not much influence with the great majority of mankind.

The rapid increase in the number of rich men was a

fact that the multitude could not reconcile with diminished wealth-producing power in the nation.

The question between the two parties, put in as few words as possible, is this: Has the wealth of our rich men been a clear addition to the wealth of the nation, or has it been at the expense of the masses? As the masses generally demand the evidence of concrete results before accepting what they have been taught to regard as mere theories, the census of 1880, now being printed, has been looked forward to as probably decisive of the whole controversy before the people.

The rumor now comes from Washington, through various channels, that the total property of the nation in 1880 was only thirty-five thousand millions. This, if nearly correct, more than confirms the most extreme calculations of the free-traders.

Let us see what the wealth of the nation should have been, and probably would have been under the revenue tariffs of 1846 and 1856.

In the decade ending 1860 the total property increased 126 per cent, and was returned, in round numbers, seventeen thousand millions. At the same rate of increase the census of 1870 would have returned thirty-eight thousand four hundred and twenty millions. The largest estimate ever made of the losses caused by the civil war were ten thousand millions. Deducting this there would remain twenty-eight thousand four hundred and twenty millions, which was about what the census made it *in currency*. At the same percentage of increase the census of 1880 would have returned sixty-four thousand two hundred and twenty-nine millions, in round numbers. This shows a reduction of productive forces amounting to over twenty-nine thousand millions in twenty years!

But this is not all. The wealth-producing power of the people *per capita* increased steadily from the adoption of the Constitution until 1860. It is not at all unreasonable to suppose it might have reached 150 per cent, under the revenue system of taxation, if not in 1870 then in 1880 at least. The loss was not in the currency. As a machine it was by far the most perfect we have ever had. It was not any defect in means of communication between producers and consumers. Railroad building has outrun population. Both inland and ocean freights have been greatly reduced; the former below the most extreme demands of the grangers of ten years ago. It is evident that there is no fault here. Where is it?

In feudal times the roads were not only very bad, but they were infested by robbers! Barons many of them; who issued from their donjons to waylay travellers.

The roads are good now. Are there any robbers on the highways of commerce? This is an age of law and order: we may therefore be sure that if robbery is practised, it is through forms of law!

Let us see if we can account for this decline in the wealth-producing forces of this great country, which Nature seems to have held in reserve for the coming of that "fulness of time" when, after a hundred generations of sages, philosophers, and poets had dreamt and written of millenniums and utopias, she could gather together on one continent people from all parts of the globe, pour into their lap all the treasures of earth, and into their brain the accumulated experience of all ages, that she might try humanity with one final experiment.

The facts I have stated in connection with steel rails and sugar are identical in essential character with all the other applications of the protective principle to legislation. Every tax of any sort is a burden upon industry, because all taxes must ultimately be paid by labor. Human ingenuity never has and never can devise any system of taxation of which this is not true.

THE EVILS OF TAXATION ARE MINIMIZED WHEN IT HAS LEAST INFLUENCE ON THE COSTS OF PRODUCTION; ITS EVILS INCREASE IN PROPORTION AS IT INCREASES THE COSTS OF PRODUCTION.

This is the subtle poison secreted by our protective tariff. It mingles with the life-blood of our whole industrial system. I have seen many arithmetical calculations of the cost of the protective tariff to the nation. I discard them, because the influence is too subtle to be treated successfully in that way. There is no branch of our national industry that does not feel this poison in its veins.

The greatest victories of human genius have been won in reducing the costs of production and in expediting transportation, and reducing its cost between producer and consumer.

True wealth consists, not in high prices, but in abundance.

If protective legislation, political, social, and commercial, had not interfered with the production and natural distribution of wealth, the discoveries and inventions of the last three to four hundred years would have accrued mainly to the benefit of labor. They would have gone far toward redeeming man from the *primeval curse*. As it is, the attempts of governments to *improve* the beneficent law of nature for private purposes have detained the masses in a state of slavery, from which their genius, applied to the utilizing of natural forces, was and is intended to redeem them.

There is another way in which "protection" reduces the wealth-producing power. It enfeebles industry.

I can with justice apply to "protection" a paraphrase of the sentiment in Homer as to slavery: The day a citizen obtains from his government "protection" against legitimate competition, he loses half his value.

This is an unknown quantity in a mere pecuniary point of view; but there is something in it above all price—manhood cannot be bought with money.

A striking example of this can be found in the history of this country during the embargo and the war of 1812. Our manufacturers, having a monopoly of the home market—being deprived of the inestimable benefit of competition, sunk into such a pitiable condition of imbecility that, at the close of the war, when English goods, made by the most advanced methods, came into our market they were as helpless as children. This caused a general cry for help from the government, which continued until the celebrated "bill of abominations," in 1828 and 1832, resulted in the nullification excitement; beginning that mortal enmity between slavery and "protection," around which for thirty years nearly all the political forces of this country crystallized.

The South was not originally opposed to "protection;" because it did not understand its economical working. The owner of a thousand slaves and ten thousand acres of land had in his bank-account an infallible guide to the influence of taxation on his interests.

An individual living by the fruit of his own labor may be taxed into pauperism without knowing the cause of his misfortune. The planter, whose whole property was in land and labor, discovered that he was being taxed through these to support rich corporations of manufacturers.

WHEN EACH BRANCH OF INDUSTRY SUPPORTS ITSELF, ALL ADD THEIR GAINS TO THE NATIONAL WEALTH; WHEN ONE INDUSTRY SUPPORTS ANOTHER, THE CONTRIBUTION IS SO MUCH DEDUCTED FROM THE AGGREGATE GAIN.

Some of my readers will be able to recall the progress of mechanical industry under the revenue tariff of 1846.

Our mercantile marine had no equal in the world. The steam-engine was covered all over with American patents.

Our inventions in agricultural implements and other labor-saving machines came before Europe like a Divine revelation.

I remember, as if it were yesterday, the first great exhibition of industry in London in 1851. I was there. It was a proud day for Americans when the victory of the yacht "America" was added to that of McCormick's reaping machine and others. The "Thunderer" in one of its rare moments, when it does justice even to the Great Republic, confessed that "America has carried off all the laurels for utilitarian inventions; that is, inventions really useful to the whole world." The multitude were wonderfully impressed. They seemed to think that nothing was impossible for Americans! I can even now feel the thrill of joy and hope that vibrated through the hearts of the liberty-loving, down-trodden masses of Europe when they beheld these laurels wreathed around the brows of Liberty and Equality!

Now our ships have left the ocean. *They are "protected."* Our hardy sailors, brave and intelligent, who in peace "wantoned with the waves" and explored every harbor on the globe; who in war carried our proud flag "into the jaws of death and into the mouth of hell," are now either in their graves, or in the service of other countries. They have no successors here, because we have no school in which to train them.

Our ship-builders: where are they? They are either in Wall Street gambling in stocks, or in the lobbies of Congress, playing some similar game. They have "*protection*," and they want more of it.

Alas, this is the direction in which "*protection*" has turned the enterprising genius of nearly all our manufacturers. If a new invention or better machinery is required, they send lobbyists to Congress to ask for an additional tax upon the whole people. If a new metal is discovered, instead of cultivating unprotected corn on the land, the owner rushes to Congress for a tax. If a speculator projects a stock company to manufacture any very important article, or to apply a discovery or invention made in Europe under the stimulus of liberty—such as Bessemer steel rails, for instance—he sends a whole lobby to Washington, perhaps composed of veteran politicians who know all the ropes. He then issues shares; not the kind of water we hear so much about, but representing solid property voted by Congress in the form of a tax. Whatever there may be in this for individuals, it is quite certain there is nothing but loss for the nation. Yet for more than ten years after the passage of the protective tariff in 1862 nearly every demand of this sort was favorably responded to by Congress.

To sum the matter up in a few words: Congress undertook through the instrumentality of taxation to supply a few manufacturers with a substitute for brains and industry. At the expense of labor a few manufacturers are enabled to live in luxury, who, without such bounty, might be forced by necessity to be themselves valuable workers, such as laborers, mechanics and farmers now are.

Another change has taken place which is very striking to those who remember the old revenue tariff, "strict construction" times. I mean the great increase of extravagance and gambling speculation in fluctuations of values. I suppose that hundreds of millions that, under the old system, would have been employed in foreign commerce, reaping from the crops of all nations to add to our own, are now employed in our

Stock and Produce Exchanges in the work of exploiting public credulity. This has already accustomed a large minority of the people to live by their wits instead of by work.

As I have already stated, the protective system includes much more than a protective tariff. It does not in this country, as in Europe, extend to land tenure, religion, and in some countries to the whole social structure; but it does include, and necessarily, a system of extravagant expenditure. It belongs to the kind of government called paternal. Hence the appropriation of public lands and even the national credit to aid in building railroads. In this way national property worth hundreds of millions became the property of gamblers.

It also includes lavish appropriations for various purposes, some of which are avowed, and some unavowed. The unavowed purposes are what concern us most.

Whether the avowed purpose be the unwise and unnecessarily rapid payment of the public debt, enormous appropriations under the name of equalization of bounties and pensions to soldiers, with openings for frauds by pension brokers and lobbyists, or the appropriations for river and harbor improvements which, though the smallest in amount, seem to attract most attention at present—I suppose on the principle that it is the last straw that breaks the camel's back—the principal unavowed purpose has been to get rid of the surplus in the treasury, and thus postpone as long as possible any reduction of taxation. There was also a minor unavowed purpose, viz.: To bribe voters with the public money. This purpose has lately been (I think, *imprudently*) acknowledged in the case of the large appropriations for Southern rivers and harbors. Another unavowed motive is the expectation of support from what are called "favored industries." This is the force which is *organized* above all others. The manufacturers having or expecting "protection" have their agents in Washington always. These agents are supplied with ample bank-credits. They make their *arguments* in the lobbies of Congress, and in the saloons and private parlors. The manufacturers control the votes of their employés through a mixture of fraud and intimidation. Over their champagne and canvas-back ducks they think they can afford to sneer at political economy and "damn the theorists."

It is the avowed purpose of "protection" to reduce imports. No increase of duties has ever accomplished this purpose for more than one year after its enactment, after which imports have always become larger than ever. There is only one way in which "protection" can permanently reduce imports, viz.: By reducing the productive forces of the country so as to impair its power to either import or export. In the end we will export as much as we will import, and import no more than we export, unless we have capital engaged in foreign commerce, when the excess of our imports will, as is the case with England, be composed of a portion or all of the profits of that commerce.

In consequence of this economic law a high tariff will generally produce excess of revenue. This is our present condition; and here comes a striking contrast between the present and the olden time.

To make way for an increase of tariff the old protectionist party, led by Henry Clay (a deluded disciple of whom I was at that time), proposed to distribute the proceeds of the public lands among the States. The economists rejected the proposal and denounced it as a fraudulent attempt to bribe the States. It was a tempting proposal; many of the Southern and Western States were very poor, and overwhelmed in debt; but some of their leaders, at least, were students of political economy. They resisted the temptation, and so branded it with infamy that it sunk in the public estimation almost to a level with the alien and sedition laws.

I state facts as I find them in such language as I deem fitting; but on no account would I have it understood that I consider all protectionists dishonest. I know the contrary. Ignorance is a far more powerful support to " protection " than interest.

Indeed I am strongly inclined to accept the opinion of Socrates, that all evil is the result of ignorance.

The influence of a high protective tariff as a fountain of corruption is well known to the initiated. It offers a premium to fraud, and places the honest importer at a fatal disadvantage. This danger was pointed out by Alexander Hamilton, the reputed father of our protective system, in an article in the *Federalist** advocating the adoption of the Constitution. He even then foresaw the danger of the system he was

---

* Article 33d.

inaugurating, and warned his countrymen to be on their guard against it. Alas for human foresight!

What our custom-houses are is well known to many who, through patriotic shame, hesitate to tell the whole truth.

American tourists in Europe can tesify that when they make purchases the sellers generally ask them at what price they wish the custom-house invoices made When told an honest invoice is required, they express surprise, and even remonstrate against such folly!

When the traveller returns, if he is honest and straightforward, he finds himself in more danger than if he were otherwise, unless he submits to be blackmailed, which he generally does rather than submit to the annoyance, vexation, and perhaps loss, which would be the certain consequence.

Those who have read Dickens' notes will remember that green spot in the dreary desert of his spiteful criticisms, in which he compliments our custom-house system, and especially the dignified courtesy of the employés; to whom the offer of a bribe seemed as much out of place as it would be to a Lord Chancellor. What a contrast to the present!

Is it reasonable to expect that the law-makers and office-holders under such a system will be always patriotic and unselfish? It is not the men, but the system, that is justly chargeable with the corruption so loudly and generally complained of.

In other times paternal government was the best possible under then existing circumstances. Under universal suffrage it is the very worst.

Look at the temptations to which the people expose their representatives, in conceding to them constitutional power to levy taxes without limit as to amount, and with such discriminations and favoritism as pleases them! The people are too busy to attend to politics, though popular government can have no reason for its existence unless they do attend to it.

Our representatives have escaped from the control of the people by disregarding the letter and spirit of the Constitution, and by enacting laws on the most important matters affecting gravely the intimate interests of the whole people, without submitting the questions to their constituents. Twice in our history protective tariffs have been foisted upon the people under the shadow of other and quite different issues that absorbed popular attention.

In the presidential canvass of 1840 the financial question was the all-absorbing issue. The charter of a national bank, for which the people voted, was defeated, and, instead, a protective tariff was enacted!

In the election of 1860, though "protection" in a very mild form was asserted in the Republican platform, the slavery question was so all-absorbing that even "incidental protection" was not so much as named in the canvass.

When the successful party took possession of the government *it was deemed expedient to conciliate the capitalists and powerful corporations by granting them special favors.* This was well understood at the time. Speculators flocked to Washington with all kinds of projects to manufacture everything under the sun, provided they were protected at the public expense.

The masses have sometimes very short memories. They have permitted this system to continue through seventeen years of peace, more than five of them years of unexampled depression and suffering!

No autocracy in the world would have dared to retain such crushing and unnecessary taxation under such circumstances!

Through all that terrible five years, and up to the present time, these protected monopolists, with the most infernal ingenuity, left no stone unturned to misdirect public attention as to the real cause of the trouble. Now it was fiat money that was needed! again it was the demonetization of silver that caused the whole trouble! It was the game of catch-thief, and the multitude, like children, followed the false scent!

In the mean time the infernal tariff remained, not because the government needed the money, for it did not, but because protected monopolists must still be conciliated ; and so long as popular attention could be successfully turned to other questions it was safe to continue the alliance with the monopolists. *This was politics.* No sharp politician will ever alienate one ally, until he makes sure of getting another! Let the people wake up and convince the politicians that they comprehend the situation, and will attend to it, and the monopolists will have to work for a living like other people.

Perhaps there is no change that has taken place in the last thirty years more striking than that in the degree of sound economical information among politicians. When the revenue tariff of 1846 passed Congress the whole question was discussed with marked ability. Robert J. Walker, the then Secretary of the Treasury, had no superior at the time, in this or any other country, as a writer on living political issues. After the passage of the revenue tariff, virtually framed by him, nearly all discussion on the subject ceased, because Mr. Walker's predictions as to its effects were more than verified by the result. The industry of the whole country was so prosperous and contented, that from 1850 to 1860 the tariff question ceased to be any longer a party issue. Unfortunately, it also passed out of the public mind, so that when the conspirators sprung it in Congress in 1861, the masses of the people knew literally nothing about it.

The decade between 1850 and 1860 was a time of wonderful industrial progress all over the world. Not only was American trade comparatively free, but England had made her trade almost entirely so. In 1842 Sir Robert Peel abolished duties on raw material; in 1846 he freed the corn trade; and within five years more the whole protective system was wiped out, including the navigation laws. English trade bounded forward and upward, like a healthy man released from fetters that had been worn from boyhood up. We were not second in the race. Our cotton crop doubled in quantity, and doubled in market price per pound. Wheat and corn increased 80 per cent in quantity, and nearly as much in price. Labor was contented—strikes were hardly ever heard of.

I remember reading an article in the New York daily *Times*, somewhere between 1856 and 1859, on an attempt being made by some immigrants to excite discontent among laborers, and to introduce trades-unions into this country. The writer treated it as an attempt to accomplish the impossible. He did not believe that European trades-unions could ever take root in our cheap land, or bear fruit in the air of freedom and equality. He stated justly that such combinations were the natural consequence of class-distinctions in society.

How does the present time compare with the past?

Well-informed, thoughtful people have often asked themselves the question, Is the ignorance of economical science manifested in high places, genuine or affected?

One party had a candidate for the Presidency who professed, in language that could hardly be misunderstood, that he knew nothing about the tariff question!

The other party had a Secretary of State, under the administration of Mr. Hayes, who undertook to use his official influence to bring about what he called "full trade," while emphatically condemning free trade!

Mr. Evarts stands too high as a man of honor to be suspected of playing with words in the discharge of a grave official trust. There is but one alternative; we must conclude that he was ignorant of the simplest rudiments and ripest axiomatic truths of economical science: worse still, that he was ignorant of that principle in the constitution of the human mind, which surely should be known to every American freeman: that NO SPHERE OF HUMAN ACTIVITY CAN EVER BE FULL UNTIL IT IS FIRST FREE.

How differently did Mr. Gladstone deal with the popular cry in England for "fair trade," which was probably a paraphrase of Mr. Evarts' "full trade." Fortunately Mr. Gladstone was a scientific economist. He brayed that fungus outgrowth of ignorance with one stamp of his foot!

Fortunate England! Unfortunate America!

How is it now in labor-strikes, trades-unions, and class-distinctions?

We have labor-strikes in abundance, and trades unions are everywhere deemed a necessity to protect one class of the community from another class, which discriminating legislation has elevated above labor.

In old times we were all "middle class," as they say in Europe. No dregs and no scum, only one clear living stream—all Americans.

Now we have scum and dregs enough. They are present to the perception of more than one of the five senses!

Could such a change have been the fruit of a system calculated to benefit working people?

I appeal to the common-sense of the work-shop and the farm for an answer. Such questions may be beneath the notice of Pennsylvania *statesmen;* the time is not far distant when the *plain people* will answer them at the ballot-box.

III.

IT IS LOW-PRICED LABOR, NOT HIGH-PRICED LABOR, THAT NEEDS "PROTECTION."

In no department of this controversy has there been so much misunderstanding, and so much successful misrepresentation, as that of the influence of free trade and " protection" on wages.

Political economists have written volumes on the subject of wages.

I think I am justified in stating that no one nor all of their theories has solved the problem. The cause of this, in my humble opinion, is the low, materialistic plane on which political economy has been treated, especially by English writers.

Adam Smith's work deserves its great reputation because of the great influence it has had in emancipating industry from legislative restrictions. It was mainly an elaborate, and even minute, sifting and verification of the best results of French studies on the wretched condition of France during the reign of Louis XV. In treating the question of wages, he seems to treat man as a minor factor. The whole work, from beginning to end, reads like a new scientific method of *fattening hogs!*

Cousin declares that political economy cannot be separated from psychology; but he was a philosopher, not an economist.

There was nobody to follow up this valuable hint. The economists were in the gutter, and could not comprehend it! Just now it begins to dawn upon thinkers that economics are, above all else, a moral science. In the time of Smith any attempt to treat social, political, and intellectual liberty as the main productive forces of a people, at least in England, would have been scouted as folly, or condemned as rank heresy.

Let us note a few facts here. I prefer to give facts first, and arguments afterward.

Wages in England are at least five times greater than in India, and 50 to 100 per cent greater than on the European continent; yet England supplies India with manufactured goods, and beats the Continent in all the markets of the world.

In cotton and grain this country meets India in the markets of Europe, and has not so much as thought of asking Congress for a bounty, though both cotton and grain pay hundreds of millions to *protect our home manufactures.*

How do our protectionist friends account for these facts? They do not even attempt a reply, because there is no theory possible that would not be fatal to "protection."

Is it not obvious that THE TRUE BAROMETER OF WAGES IS THE DEGREE IN WHICH LABOR IS PRODUCTIVE?

The inferior mental, social, and political condition of the two hundred millions of India makes labor there worth precisely what it commands—that is, almost nothing.

"Protection" in this country, and in France and Germany, not only secures England from all danger of competition in the open markets of the world, BUT BY DEPRIVING HER RIVALS OF THE INESTIMABLE BENEFIT OF FREE COMPETITION, IS SLOWLY BUT SURELY WEAKENING THEIR PRODUCTIVE FORCES.

Ten years more of high "protection" would make it a hard struggle, without positive prohibition, to retain control of their home markets. The failure of the French bounty system to ship-owning and building will, sooner or later, cover that branch of the protective system with ridicule.

From the above facts, which are known to everybody, it is evident that it is high-priced labor, and not low-priced labor, that is really formidable.

Ask an English, Scotch, or Irish mechanic who worked at his trade at home, and afterward in this country for a series of years, and he will tell you that a mechanic here gets through with 50 to 100 per cent more work than he had ever known in the same number of hours in Europe.

I have asked this question repeatedly, with substantially the same reply. Incredulous at first, I inquired whether this was not entirely owing to labor-saving machinery. The reply was—no, not at all. An intelligent gentleman who came to this country as a journeyman tailor, and is now wealthy, told me it was so in his trade when he first arrived here, and without the use of machinery.

I lately made the same inquiry of an American master-mechanic of high standing in this city. He confirmed the others in every particular, and added that he had known competent mechanics from Europe, after arriving here, offer their services for little more than half wages for a year, in order to learn the secret. An English master-workman, who travelled in this country to look into our industrial progress and report the result to his fellow-workers at home, used this language in his report: "You will never be able to understand the report of what I saw, unless you first know what it is for people to be *set on fire by liberty.*"

European labor soon catches this fire when it reaches our shores, and breathes our spiritual atmosphere. IT IS NOT IN EUROPE THAT EUROPEAN LABOR IS FORMIDABLE; IT IS AFTER IT ARRIVES HERE!

What an anomaly it is, this Samson sleeping in the lap of "protection," which is shearing him of his strength! This giant deliberately putting fetters on his own limbs!

I am addressing workers. I wish to speak eye to eye and face to face with the men who work in the factory, the workshop, on the road, in the forest, and on the farm, the men who PRODUCE ALL THE WEALTH, AND PAY ALL THE TAXES. The men who constitute the real American Republic, its genius, its virility, its sole hope in the future. Overflowing with vital force, they sometimes run into fearful errors, that would be fatal to an inferior race; but so splendidly do they recover from their mistakes, that the gain seems to outweigh the loss.

I ask you to consider for a moment who and what you are, and what are your surroundings—in short, what your allotment is in the order of Divine Providence.

Never did the same number of civilized, educated people possess such an area of fertile land. Its mineral is only second to its agricultural richness.

The interests of labor are inseparably connected with land. Cheap land means a cheap tool for the worker; but it means more, it is both a stimulus and an encouragement. It offers newer and greater opportunities in other departments of industry. A new machine is invented: it increases production, and adds to the general well-being. But this is not all; these bounties of nature and victories of mind educate and develop manhood. This seems to be the purpose of nature.

"Wealth has its origin in the application of mind to nature."* This consists in understanding her laws, and co-operating with them. The whole history of man on earth is a continual struggle with Nature to wrest her secrets from her. She refuses her favors to everything but force; but she longs to be conquered. She tests and trains her wooer with all sorts of fortune. A hundred times she tests his mettle by disappointment; once she encourages him by success. Oh! she so delights in making strong men! It is only into the ears of such she will reveal her secrets.

"Wealth is not primarily the result of industry,

---

* Emerson.

much less of economy, but of knowing, and co-operating with natural forces."*

The world belongs to the man who knows. Knowledge is the richness of all riches! Nature is a strict economist. She holds rewards in one hand and penalties in the other. When she produces two bushels of wheat instead of one, she offers it as an opportunity to her children. If they respond by inventing a machine that will increase production tenfold, or an hundredfold, her blessings are without reserve; if, on the contrary, the opportunity is used for idle indulgence, her blessings are turned to curses.

It is not the purpose of Nature to feed and fatten men like hogs. She intends man to be her master—the master of all things.

To assert that the price of land is the standard of wages belittles the whole question. Moreover, it is not true. When a few Indians owned this whole continent, and land was surely cheap enough, what was wages? Of course this is an extreme case, but extreme cases expose false theories.

The true barometer of wages is liberty. Minds emancipated by real education; industry freed from all legislative interference, as in the interior trade of this Union; all political and social inequalities wiped out, and all barriers to personal force, excepting only a just respect for the rights of others, removed entirely.

This view of political economy can hardly be expected to be very popular among educated people in England at present.

---

* Emerson.

England has admitted liberty into her trade, but her wealthy classes are fighting hard to keep liberty of trade from suggesting to the people their need of liberty in other things. The struggle will be vain.

Her land tenure, primogeniture, and mediæval class distinctions, which are an insult to nineteenth century humanity, and a disgrace to the nineteenth century people who permit them to exist, will be revolutionized by the leaven of free trade.

Already she has found that, in order to maintain her supremacy in commerce, she must educate her labor. I learn that this policy has been adopted even in India. What a glorious triumph this is for economical science! It elevates it into the purest atmosphere of ethics! Nor is this the only point at which it touches, and co-operates with, the purest moral sentiment.

It is a demonstrated truth in economics that the good of each is best for all.

The idea that ruled Europe for three hundred years from the accession of Charles V. to the throne, that whatever is gained by one party in trade is at the expense of some other, is exploded forever.

Thus the law of love, which religious believers regarded as a dogma, and unbelievers as a Pickwickian kind of truth, is demonstrated to be an immutable law of nature.

Do not understand me as regarding what is called the land question as unimportant. The protective system has already alienated an immense area of the public domain, without any necessity, or any compensating advantage to the people.

Reform in land legislation is only second to freedom of trade. To be effective it must be in the direction of in-dividualism, which is the spirit of this age. It should, as far as possible, prevent the ownership of land by any other than actual cultivators. This should be the main point aimed at, but must not be attempted by violating the principles of justice. Injustice never can cure any evil greater than the evils it will produce.

It is generally believed that abstract economical science has had very little influence on practical legislation. This belief has some foundation in fact, and I think is mainly owing to the low level on which its authors and advocates have treated it.

Modern political economy had its birth in France. As might be expected, English and Scotch economists treated the subject on a lower plane, and with a narrower range of intellectual sympathies than the French.

English political and social philosophy, when touched by sentiment, rarely ventures beyond feeding and clothing the masses, making them contented with their lot, *and saving their souls.* A good work surely; who can doubt it? But it leaves out nearly all that distinguishes mind from matter. There is no inspiration in it, and no enthusiasm. But that is not all; and this lesson physical science must learn sooner or later: it is fatal to anything like complete science!

It is only the lowest note in the gamut. Mental evolution, aspiration, individualism and its natural concomitant human solidarity, instead of being the emphasis, the chorus of the science, are barely touched. Science must sweep the chords of the whole musical scale in all its octaves before it can reach universal harmony, which is the analogue of synthesis in science.

The first school of economical science was the offspring of that indescribable wretchedness and misery which finally produced the French Revolution. The father of this school was François Quesney. As I am now writing for workingmen, I will state who this splendid specimen of a self-educated workingman was.

He worked on his father's farm, and was not even taught to read and write. He was, however, a born genius, with a passionate desire for knowledge.

"The things men desire most in their youth, come to them in troops in their old age."* So it was with Quesney.

The disadvantages arising from lack of early education were counterbalanced by freedom from the bondage of formulas. He did not have to waste half his life in extricating himself from those grooves which connect so many educational institutions with the age of darkness.

Louis XV. called him "the thinker," and lodged him in his palace. Some of his fundamental maxims are worth recording, because they are true and always applicable.

"He found that the law of nature is the supreme law, and that social and political laws must conform to it. He found a correlation between physical and moral laws so close that, if either be misunderstood

---
* Jean Paul.

through ignorance or passion, the others are also. He found that matter bears to mankind very much the relation which body does to soul. Hence, that natural justice is the conformity of human laws and actions to natural order. He argued: if these laws exist, our intelligence is capable of understanding them, and all men and all States ought to be governed by them. Instinct conforms to intelligence. Every one is endowed with the triple instincts of well-being, sociability, and justice. The isolation of the brute is not suitable to the double nature of man. The idea of liberty and the idea of property are practically inseparable, because liberty includes the right of man to the fruit of his labor. Among fundamental rights he placed freedom of person, freedom of opinion, and freedom of contract, or exchange. Among general maxims he declared the fallacy of the doctrine of the balance of trade. He says: let entire freedom of commerce be maintained, both internal and external. The policy most sure, most true and most profitable to the nation, and to the State, exists in entire freedom of competition."* This is the foundation of the science of political economy. Quesney died in 1774, while Turgot, his most illustrious disciple, was making, as Prime Minister of France, his first experiments in liberating trade, by establishing complete freedom of the corn trade in France, both internal and external.

It will be remembered that the first move in the same direction in England was the law freeing the corn trade sixty-two years afterward. This is doubly

---

* Macleod.

significant. It shows, what all the records of the time demonstrate, that these first practical applications of liberty were forced by starvation, and it shows, also, the terribly destructive influence of protective legislation on human happiness.

"Governments," says Turgot, "are apt to immolate the well-being of the individual to the pretended right of society. They forget that society is only made for individuals, and that it is only instituted to protect the right of all, in insuring the performance of mutual duties."

You see how closely all rights, and the liberty to exercise them, are united together. If you attempt to separate them, you prevent the circulation of the very life-blood of liberty. FREE TRADE WILL IN TIME LIBERATE THE WHOLE MAN. WITHOUT LIBERTY OF TRADE, ALL OTHER LIBERTY IS A MOCKERY.

The perfect freedom of trade and intercourse between the States, in all their vast territory and varied productions, is probably worth more in practical value to the whole people of the United States, than any other provision in the Constitution!—*and fortunately this provision is in plain language.*

Such was the effect of liberating the corn trade in France, that Pitt made a treaty with Turgot in 1786, based upon a fair degree of reciprocal freedom. Pitt also made a strenuous effort to liberate the trade of Ireland. He had been a close student of Adam Smith's work, then ten years old.

His attempt raised a storm of prejudice and ignorant

selfishness. One incident of that exciting time is worth recording.

Josiah Wedgewood, the celebrated pottery manufacturer, waited on Pitt with a remonstrance against bringing English labor into equal competition with the *pauper labor* of Ireland. When he got through Mr. Pitt replied: "Mr. Wedgewood, you are an excellent manufacturer of pottery, but you are a very poor statesman."

What a loss to this country that we have not had a Pitt on our tariff commission.

Pitt's attempts to emancipate industry were all thwarted by the passions aroused by the French Revolution. They were, in their origin, mainly a religious frenzy, stimulated by the mad genius of Burke; but they rapidly grew into a positive hatred toward liberty of all kinds. These wars threw back civilization, not fifty years, as Byron supposed, but a hundred years. Still it was the economical truths Pitt learned from Adam Smith that enabled England to bear and to survive the tremendous strain of twenty years of war, in which she either fought or subsidized half the Continent.

The affinity between war and restrictive legislation on commercial intercourse between nations has often been noticed. The essential, germinal motive-power is the same in both, but there is this difference—mark it well:

WAR IS A GREAT WICKEDNESS; "PROTECTION" IS A GREAT MEANNESS!

In the economy of Nature great wickedness is often

utilized, and made fruitful of good ; whereas meanness is so obnoxious to Nature, that she has given it but one power—that of self-destruction. She places along the bloody pathway of war some of the noblest virtues, to be nourished and promoted thereby. The cowardice of "protection" has no redeeming force in it.

IV.
APPEAL TO WORKINGMEN.

I wish to bring this whole question before the people who are most directly interested in it: the farmers, mechanics and laborers—the men who produce all the wealth and enjoy least of the luxuries; the men who pay all the taxes and do most of the voting. These are the men who suffer most from bad legislation, and yet have the indisputable power to correct it.

A word of advice, my friends. Let us be candid. Feeling every throb of your hearts and breathing the very atmosphere of your aspirations, I claim the right to talk to you as brothers.

Don't you think you spend too much time at corner groceries and in political caucuses, trying to elect your inferiors to make laws for you? These men know no more about your true interests than you do yourselves, and, unfortunately, they care much less. They will nearly always address your passions much more than your judgment. Beware of the man who appeals to your party prejudices, no matter for what purpose. The more you listen to such demagogism, the less you will know.

Now permit me to make a suggestion as to the course which, I think, you should pursue.

Instead of wasting your time and energies doing the

work of slaves for politicians, you should organize lyceums, where you can meet and discuss your own interests, in a sober, rational manner, as becomes American citizens. From these lyceums whiskey and party politics should be rigidly excluded. You can make them radiating centres of light and power.

Depend upon it, my friends, your most imminent, pressing contest is not with capital, but with ignorance. Against this wage a war of extermination—and at once! Devote your workingman's lyceums to reading, discussion, and debate. In this way you will not only acquire knowledge, but also learn how to express it forcibly.

When workingmen, thus equipped, enter the halls of legislation, directly from the workshops, the lawyers who now govern us will begin to retire—reality will take the place of sham.

I would have you cease voting for lawyers as if they were divinely appointed to be your masters, and learn that you yourselves are not only their masters, but the masters of all.

Nor will your countrymen regret the change, if you will first equip yourselves with knowledge suitable to the task.

You will find economical science broad enough and deep enough to cover all your interests. I will try to sum up, in as few words as possible, the essential lessons which I think are taught by the historical review I have attempted. You can discuss them at your leisure; but be sure you do it thoroughly. I will be delighted if you can meet in your own lyceums to do so.

I.

The first fact demonstrated in the review is the natural and historical connection between slavery and "protection." Their antagonism was also natural; it was a quarrel over the spoils of labor.

I thought I had completed the parallel between them, but since I began, Judge Kelley, the leading representative of the "infant industries," has appeared in the character of a protectionist *fire-eater*, notifying the country that if the internal revenue system be not abolished, we will have civil war! Who could imagine that the Representative of the Quaker City would repeat the rôle of Wm. L. Yancey, breathing threatenings and slaughter, if the government dares to withhold its *milk ration from the Pennsylvania nursery?* Taxes that are collected by the government are not the kind of taxes the protectionists want.

The laws of historical development are fatal, and will, no doubt, continue so to the end. Slavery almost ruined the Democratic party. When "protection" does the same work for the Republican party, then, and not till then, will the nation be free and the people contented. Among the most contented citizens will be the protectionists themselves. On the whole, they are not so much to blame for their present false position. They have become involved in a network of sophistries, from which they are powerless to extricate themselves. Their countrymen must come to their aid.

Our brethren of the South are well content to have the negro free. It is a great mistake to imagine they would willingly return to the old system. They have found that the colored man is a much more productive factor in industrial progress as a freeman than as a slave. Besides, he stands on his own feet, and must himself reap what he sows—rewards, or penalties. This is justice; and when justice is done, everybody is relieved and happy.

You will find this a fruitful fountain of information, from which to draw in your lyceum discussions.

II.

The second fact demonstrated is that "protection" thwarts the just and beneficent law of nature, which ordains that every man shall reap the fruit of his own labor. Be well assured that when you see one portion of the community systematically reaping the fruits of the toil of the rest, the fault is not in the Almighty power that rules the universe. The fault is in man himself, who is not content with the natural law of justice.

When dealing with this branch of the subject, it is difficult to suppress a feeling of passionate indignation. Still, I trust it will be approached with the calmness and dignity which its gravity and importance deserves.

Enlightened selfishness, if I may use the expression, is an indispensable force in all human progress; it is probably most powerful in the most active and progressive communities; and hence most liable to become aggressive and to forget justice.

Nobles and paupers do not properly belong to an industrial age. They are a legacy from barbarism. In the ages of darkness, society naturally divided itself into patrons and clients; into alms-givers and alms-receivers.

It is the mission of this positive, industrial, scientific age to solve this great problem of poverty and riches, so as to substitute justice for alms. It is not enough to feed the poor; they must be restored to a consciousness of the dignity of manhood. Otherwise, alms are twice cursed; they curse him who gives, and him who receives. They destroy the natural relations between man and his fellow-man, germinating the fruitful root of all anarchy.

I think I have shown with sufficient clearness what it is that has, within twenty years, filled our woods with tramps and our streets with beggars, and is constantly producing wider and wider divisions in American society. Do you imagine that you can, with impunity, be indifferent to the misfortunes of your fellow-workers? Are you quite sure that the next revulsion in trade will not drive you also into vagabondism?

Depend upon it, my friends, it is you alone who can solve this problem. If you leave it to lawyers and politicians the disease, which is now gnawing at the vitals of the Republic, will soon be past cure.

III.

I have shown that "protection" reduces the wealth-producing power of the nation more than one half. With free-trade, or anything nearly approaching it, there would be, to-day, at least $600 more property than there is, for each man, woman, and child in the United States. If the wealth of the millionaires was a clear addition to the wealth of the country, it would be presumptive evidence that it is the just reward of their own genius and industry; as it is, there can be no doubt as to how it was obtained.

How all this has been brought about I have shown in part, but the subject is inexhaustible.

Take the single article of iron. A tax on iron increases the cost of production in every single department of civilized industry. This increase goes on augmenting in percentage, from the simplest blacksmith's work to the most complex productions of the artisan. A direct bounty paid out of the national treasury, compared to the present system, by which the *bounty* is added to the price of the article, would not cost the nation one dollar in a hundred of what it now costs. If you will follow out the investigation in this direction, you will find abundant demonstration that, of all forms of taxation, that which increases most the cost of commodities, is the most injurious to industry. I do not make the usual distinction between what is called raw materials, and other commodities. I have never been able to draw any definite line between them. Iron, in all stages of its manufacture, from the ore in the mine to the ploughs and harrows and threshing machines on the farm, to the steam-engine, the cotton-spindles in the mills, and the pumping-engine in the mine, is, properly considered, the raw material of the trade in which it is used.

I can safely leave this line of investigation to the farmers and mechanics. They have at hand ample material from which to calculate how much "protection" costs them. They may also profitably employ their leisure evenings in trying to estimate in how much better condition they would be, if twenty-nine thousand millions were added to the national wealth, and distributed according to the laws of natural justice.

IV.

I have, I think, demonstrated that it is low-priced labor, and not high-priced labor, that needs "protection," and that this must be in the form of liberty and education, which cannot be separated; the one without the other being worthless for any high purpose.

IN CIVILIZED SOCIETY EVERY HUMAN BEING BROUGHT INTO THE WORLD HAS A RIGHT TO BE EDUCATED AT THE PUBLIC EXPENSE.

Let that sentence be printed in letters of gold in every one of your lyceums.

The progress of the human mind toward its own emancipation, and its mastery over natural forces, is furnishing a new field for the development of economical science. It is already approaching the point at which a true science of mental dynamics will begin to unfold itself, and ultimately become the keystone of the whole structure. I will now try a simple, and altogether a practical line of discussion, that, if followed up, will lead to a rich field of discovery in this direction.

Land and capital are admitted, on all hands, to be important factors in determining the price of labor. Let us consider what are the elements in land and capital that enter into the question of labor.

Land requires lines of communication and means of

transportation to make it valuable. Formerly there was little mind employed in furnishing these; now there is a great deal. Land at the present time, without the railroad and the steamship, and the agricultural machinery, which are mostly the fruits of American inventive genius, would be worth very little.

You can see that three fourths of all that makes land valuable proceeds directly from the human mind.

How is it about capital? The greatest achievement of modern industrial enterprise is the development of credit. Without this, the other discoveries would have been, if not impossible, at least comparatively fruitless.

If you will watch the financial reports from day to day, and from week to week, you will find that at least 99 per cent. of what is called capital is really credit. Be sure you get upon the files of your lyceums all authentic reports from the banks, the clearing-houses, and the stock and other exchanges. There is knowledge in them worth much to you, if you know how to use it.

You have hitherto looked upon these gigantic financial operations as far away from you as the heavens are from the earth. You ask, How are we to command capital? I answer, By association and by character. If you have well deserved confidence in each other, your little savings will be enough for the nucleus, around which credit will crystallize rapidly. All the capital in the world will be at your command as soon as you convince the world that it is safe in your hands. Why should you not control your own industry, and obtain from it a just share of its rewards, instead of, as now, getting merely a pittance?

Depend upon it, this cannot be done if you follow politicians in a vain search for benefit from unequal and unjust legislation.

It cannot be done by legislation at all. I would have you understand that you are the masters of your own destiny.

When you understand this whole question, as you will if you follow up the lyceum system I propose, you will know that, when a politician proposes to you to benefit workingmen by levying a tax, direct or indirect, especially the latter, he is either a knave or a fool.

You will also learn on this point that you cannot afford to lose any time; that not only wise legislation involving your rescue from pauperizing taxation, but the real productiveness and compensation of your labor depends upon your own intelligence. It is through intelligence you can render the most valuable service to mankind, and it is in proportion to the value of that service you will be compensated, provided you will prohibit all government interference, and make industry absolutely free; always remembering that true freedom and justice are convertible terms. When the one may not be used for the other, it defines it. With these hints I leave the subject in your hands.

V.

With regard to the Land Question a few words will be sufficient.

In this country we have free trade in land: in England land is protected as rigidly as trade and navigation were fifty years ago. The sale and transfer of land there is obstructed as importation is in our own custom-houses.

Our danger is mainly in the future. The public domain is rapidly passing into private ownership, in one way or another. The time is not distant when capitalists will invest in land, not on speculation, as now, but to rent it out to workers. This has been the curse of Europe, and should be prevented at all hazards but one—viz. a violation of the principles of justice.

It is for you, my friends, to solve the problem as to how this can be done.

Until it is done, American freedom will never be established on a durable foundation.

VI.

I have shown that there was, in revenue tariff times, a larger proportion of the population engaged in productive industries, and fewer in idleness and gambling, than under the present high tariff.

The decade from 1850 to 1860 was not by any means a prosperous time for speculators. It was all the more so for workers; and the progress of the nation in wealth was correspondingly great.

Remember, the number of idlers in a community is not a matter of indifference to workingmen. Every idler is a burden on labor, and must be supported by it.

These idlers and gamblers are a much greater burden on labor than if they were openly acknowledged paupers, because they consume much more.

This leads directly to the consideration of another burden which "protection" puts upon the back of labor.

VII.

I have shown that "protection" increases the cost of production in every department of industry, thereby lowering the net compensation of the worker, and effectually excluding our manufactures from the markets of the world. When a surplus is produced beyond the requirements of the home market, the only choice we have is between exporting at a loss and discharging the workmen.

Both expedients were resorted to during the depression following the panic of 1873. If our industry had been on a natural basis, our productions would have flowed out into the markets of the world as our rivers flow into the ocean, without the slightest disturbance to the universal equilibrium. As it was, a large part of our working people were doomed to idleness. This, with the other baneful influences of "protection," reduced the value of the wealth-producing forces of the nation during the decade, from thirty thousand millions, which it should have been, to about thirteen thousand millions. The working people of the nation had not only to lose all this out of their earnings, but al so *to contribute toward enriching many millionaires.*

In the mean time the public domain is being given away to European immigrants, the "pauper laborers" we hear so much about. Half a million to a million of them are pouring in each year, to take possession of this free gift of *our wonderfully liberal government*, while our "protectionist" writers and orators are singing pæans to the victories of "protection," which, they say, is attracting the labor of the world to the Republic!

This is surely the audacity of past impunity.

I ask the working people, once for all, to put an end to that impunity, by showing that they understand it. I do not doubt that any nation in Europe, even the most "effete despotism," could attract immigrants, by offering to them as a free gift the property of their people.

You will have work for your lyceums in breaking through the network of sophistry, and the mountains of rhetoric furnished by the rich treasuries of the "protectionists."

VIII.

I have shown that the prolific fountain from which has flowed nearly all the corruptions and irregularities in government, from which the nation has from time to time suffered, ever since the formation of the Union, was the loose methods of constitutional interpretation arising out of the compromise between slavery and "protection"; or, more correctly, the inferential yielding of the convention to slavery and to "protection," in order to conciliate them, and so render union possible on some terms.

It will surprise most people to find that there is not in the letter of the Constitution any power whatever granted to Congress to pass a protective tariff, or any form of tax whatever that the government does not itself collect, and appropriate, to pay its constitutional expenses.

Active " protection" to slavery and to manufacturers rests upon a kind of interpretation which, if followed out in other directions, would put Congress in possession of *absolute power*. Do not deceive yourselves, my friends. If you leave an opening in the Constitution large enough for a lawyer to put his hand into, he will soon make it big enough to drive in a coach and four.

Powerful governments always obtain from the judiciary whatever decisions they require to carry out their purposes: whether it is Louis Napoleon moulding the French judiciary to his purpose as if it were wax; the English ministry asking the opinion of the law officers of the Crown as to their power to stop Confederate cruisers; the Democratic party demanding from the Supreme Court a decision on the Dred Scott case, or the Republican party reorganizing the Supreme Court to prevent an adverse decision on the constitutionality of the Legal Tender act: it is always and everywhere the same.

Protectionists have not given much attention to the Constitution of late years. They have locked up the book with a golden key; not that they objected to its use in certain kinds of cases, such as the right of freedmen to vote, etc. Indeed, they were willing to aid in enforcing the Constitution *in all but one of its departments*.

When the Constitution was appealed to in economical questions—when taxes were levied, and money appropriated from the public treasury—" protection " not only sneered at it, but in some cases went so far as to denounce it as "incipient treason."

I know the lawyers will tell you that the Constitution must be construed according to precedent, and according to the intentions of its framers; at least this is what they say when it suits the purpose in hand.

At another time they will tell you that the intentions of the framers of a law cannot be inquired into by the courts, so as to change the obvious meaning of the language of the law itself. As to the authority of precedent, you will find the court always ready to make a new precedent when it thinks it sees reason for doing so.

Slavery and "protection" have changed the *golden* sentences of the Constitution into *india rubber*.

It is only by destroying the cause that you can get rid of its consequences. Slavery is gone: that is one enemy less. Now, all you have to do is to demand a strict adherence to the letter of the Constitution in taxation and expenditure, and by this simple act you will bury "protection" in the same grave with slavery.

YOUR RIGHT TO SELL THE PRODUCTS OF YOUR LABOR IN THE DEAREST MARKET, AND TO BUY WHAT YOU NEED IN THE CHEAPEST MARKET, WITHOUT OBSTRUCTIVE INTERFERENCE FROM YOUR GOVERNMENT, IS A NATURAL RIGHT, WHICH CANNOT, IN A CONSTITUTIONAL GOVERNMENT, BE ALIENATED BY INFERENCE.

IX.

We have now arrived at the point of practical politics when we must answer the question, What action does the present position demand from the American people? I have praised the so-called revenue tariffs of 1846 and 1856 because they were timely and in the right direction. On no account would I advise a return to the principles on which these tariffs were framed. There are two very good reasons for rejecting such a policy, either one of which is fatal.

In the first place, such a course would leave open the constitutional question of the right of Congress to levy unequal taxation, by a tariff giving one dollar to the revenue and three dollars to favored industries. We must return to the letter of the Constitution at once.

The constitutional convention yielded to the threats of slavery and "protection" so far as to permit them such latitude of interpretation as might conciliate them to the Union, yet without any specific sanction of their demands.

In the whole course of human history there is no more startling commentary on the *danger of yielding to threats!* The world knows what slavery cost the nation.

It is not yet generally known that "protection" has cost a great deal more than slavery, not only in a pecuniary point of view, but morally.

Henry Clay, when driven by the constitutional argument from the undisguised demand for "protection," invented that phrase, "A tariff for revenue, with incidental protection." If this means anything, it means *a law that protects without the knowledge of its enactors.* A system that drives great statesmen and orators like

Clay to such quibbling as this poisons the fountains of legislation.

Webster was, at heart, a free trader, but when forced by his constituents to defend "protection," did not dare to defend the principle. He said to Calhoun, "You advocated the tariff in 1816; I opposed it. Through 'protection' against my wish, you have built up industries that you have no right to abandon." This is the "vested interest" argument, which even Senator Bayard respects sufficiently to make him yield ground on the tariff question.

When Sir Robert Peel was replying to the free traders in Parliament in 1842, he used this language—I quote from memory: "If I were legislating for a new country, I would adopt the free-trade principle without hesitation, but in an old country like England there are vested interests that cannot be disregarded." Within five years after, they *were* disregarded; and they seem to have got along wonderfully well!

Of course every corruptionist in the land will oppose a strict construction of the Constitution. This will be his *last ditch;* if driven from every other line of battle, he will die here. He knows well that if this door is left open, he can return again when the people are asleep.

This question would have been settled definitely in the time of Calhoun but for one thing: slavery dared not state the whole constitutional question, because in doing so it would have taken away the ground from under its own feet, though slavery had much more footing in the Constitution than "protection." I repeat, there is no safety for the liberties and well-being of the nation until "protection" is eliminated from the tariff, and the constitutional barrier to such legislation is defined.

But there is another reason for rejecting the principle of the Robert J. Walker tariff at the present time, equally fatal to it. Five years before the outbreak of the civil war the Walker tariff began to be insufficient.

The repeal of the navigation laws by England in 1848 was one of the finest exhibitions of scientific statesmanship on record. The modifications in these laws accomplished by Huskisson in 1825 and 1826, proving beneficial, English statesmen were quick to learn the lesson. Notwithstanding the fact that our mercantile marine was gaining on that of England every year, and continued to gain until 1855, yet her Parliament completed the work of liberating her people from government meddling by opening even the coasting trade to the equal competition of the whole world in 1854. Now mark what followed.

This country could beat the world so long as ships were built of *untaxed timber*.

It was no *accident* that iron ship-building was pushed forward into competition with wood, with all the resources and appliances of scientific and mechanical genius. Rather it was the kind of *accident* that always happens to genuine manhood when thrown upon its own resources, under the stimulus of ambition and rivalry.

When a certain Roman consul found his army confronted with an overwhelming force of barbarians, he discovered that they had a superstitious custom which, on a certain day, would render them unfit for defence. He manœuvred until that day arrived, when he attacked and destroyed their whole army.

England discovered that we had a *fetich*, called iron. Nature had given to us more iron than to all Europe put together. Instead of using it as a servant we worshipped it as a *god*, with great temples and a numerous priesthood maintained at the public expense! They calculated correctly. Rather than give up our pet superstition, we relinquished the commercial empire of the world!

When iron began to displace wood in ship-building, true statesmanship would have instantly freed it from all taxation of every sort.

IT IS NOW TOO LATE TO TALK ABOUT MODIFICATIONS OF THE PROTECTIVE SYSTEM.

If England was hampered by any degree of "protection," we might do so.

Nature made this continent and people, with all the resources necessary to command the commerce of the world. If we would fulfil our destiny we must *carry no weights*.

England has had more than thirty years of perfect freedom in trade—open-air competition with the whole world. She has been breathing the atmosphere of the hurricane and the cyclone, while we have been coddling ourselves in the nursery. For thirty years she has been strenuously exerting all her intellectual resources to reduce the cost of production, while all our economical legislation has been in the opposite direction.

We have still great advantages, not only in material resources, but in education and in social and political liberty. Let us use these advantages while we can. This century will not be completed without a revolution in England—peaceful, because it will be the work of economical science, whose works are all peaceful. The necessities of trade rivalry will force England to educate and free her people. When *we* enter the arena, these necessities will permit of no delay.

Here I am met by the question, How is the necessary revenue to be raised? Nothing can be simpler.

Levy import duties in such a way as to minimize the cost of production. To do this the protective principle must be rigidly excluded. For instance, any import duty on iron is necessarily protective, and increases the cost of everything produced, either in the workshop or on the farm. A duty on coffee or tea minimizes the evil. Plenty of revenue can be raised without taxing the many for the support of the few. Under a strictly revenue system, manufacturers will have all their raw material at a minimum cost, and workingmen will get their clothing and their tools at half their present price. Farmers will have their expenses also reduced one half, leaving them that much more to divide with their hired laborers.

With an honest purpose there will be no difficulty in raising necessary revenue, and also in reducing the expenses of the government almost one half.

Now, my friends, I will conclude for the present with a final word of advice.

Politics are much decried by dilettanti and snobs.

For you they are of incalculable importance. What good does voting do you, unless you know what you are voting for? You have been going to the ballot-box too long like flocks of sheep to the slaughter-pen!

Do not depend on others any longer for information on matters that vitally concern yourselves *above all others*. I think that more can be done to promote the happiness and well-being of a larger number of human beings through politics than through any other instrumentality at present.

Read the life of Benjamin Franklin, and learn from him how to cultivate your minds and the minds of your fellow-workers, by meeting together evenings to discuss questions of interest, to read and debate. See to it that you have several copies of his life and works in every one of your lyceums or clubs.

www.ingramcontent.com/pod-product-compliance
Lightning Source LLC
Chambersburg PA
CBHW022148090426
42742CB00010B/1428